Animal Habitats

The Lizard in the Jungle

Text by Mike Linley

Photographs by Oxford Scientific Films

Methuen Children's Books
in association with Belitha Press

Contents

Note : The use of a capital letter for a lizard's name indicates that it is a *species* of lizard (ie Komodo Dragon) and the use of lower case means that it is a member of a larger *group* of lizards.

The Green Iguana is one of the largest lizards in the jungle.

The Plumed Basilisk spends most of its time high up in the trees.

Lizards in the jungle

Lizards are *reptiles,* relatives of the snakes and tortoises. Reptiles are cold-blooded and rely on the sun to keep warm, and so most of them are found in the world's warmer regions.

There are 3,750 known *species* of lizard in the world. Of the sixteen main groups, five are normally found in *tropical* forests or jungles. They are the iguanas, medium and large lizards that live in trees and are often *herbivorous*; the geckoes, usually small *nocturnal* lizards that eat insects; the chameleons, strange-looking lizards that change colour and can catch insects with their long sticky tongues; the agamas, often similar to iguanas but mainly *insectivorous*; and the skinks, small to medium-sized lizards with very smooth scales and short legs.

Iguanas are only found in the Americas and Madagascar, agamas everywhere except the Americas, chameleons live in Southern Europe, Africa and Asia and geckoes and skinks are found worldwide.

Choose any one tree in the jungle and you could well find a dozen or more different types of lizard living on, in or under it. The 'jungles', or hot, tropical forests, of the world are home to more species of lizard than anywhere else on earth. Especially the jungles of Central America. Every part of the forest is home to lizards of one sort or another. Burrowing lizards live in the warm, moist soil around the roots of the trees. Tiny skinks dart between the fallen leaves and a whole variety of geckoes, anoles and agamas live on the trunks, while in the upper branches live larger vegetarian lizards such as iguanas. There are also some species which move about from one area to another. The tree-living lizards have strong sharp claws for climbing or special pads on their feet.

The temperature in the jungle is more or less the same all year round, there are no seasons as we know them. The only thing that varies during the year is the rainfall. This means that jungle-living lizards are active all year round – they don't have to spend months *hibernating* as they do in *temperate* regions. It also means that it's warm enough for them to breed most of the year round too.

3

The Little Barking Gecko emerges from its desert burrow at night to hunt for food.

Lizards around the world

With the exception of the North and South Poles, lizards are found throughout the world. In the Americas they can be found from Canada all the way down to the very tip of the South American continent – Tierra del Fuego. One species, the Common or Viviparous Lizard, survives in Norway within the Arctic Circle. But lizards are great sun-lovers, so the nearer you travel to the *equator*, the more numerous they become.

Most lizards are found in tropical areas and virtually every species lives on land. Most are out and about by day but some, like the geckoes and night lizards, live in places where it's warm enough to be active at night. In hot deserts lizards are usually only active for a few hours in the early morning and late afternoon. During the middle of the day it's far too hot for them and they hide away in the cool of a bush, under a stone or in a burrow. Lizards need the sun to keep warm. In the tropics this is not a problem but in cooler areas it can be. In temperate zones, lizards are restricted to *habitats* where they can get lots of sunshine – sunny banks, heaths, dry walls and sand dunes.

Many islands around the world – even those hundreds of miles (kms) from the nearest land – have lizards. This is probably because lizards 'raft' very well. That means that they can spend many weeks without food or water, drifting out at sea on a log or floating mat of vegetation, before being washed up on some remote island or coral reef.

But the ideal places for lizards are the tropical forests – the jungles of the tropics. They are hot and humid and teeming with wildlife of every sort.

The Fringe-toed Lizard has special scales on its toes that allow it to run over the loose sand.

Many lizards have tails that are three, sometimes four times the length of their bodies.

The lizard's body

Like all reptiles, lizards are cold-blooded; that is, they can't produce their own body heat like mammals and birds do. But their bodies will only work properly at a certain temperature – about the same body temperature as ourselves. This is why lizards are restricted to the warmer parts of the earth where they have access to lots of sunshine. Lizards rely on the sun to keep warm. The first thing they do in the morning is to flatten themselves out in the warmth of the sun's rays and once they are warm enough they can run around and feed. As they begin to cool down they stop again to warm up. The cooler the day, the longer the lizard has to spend basking.

Skinks have round bodies and smooth scales, so they can slither through the undergrowth.

Most lizards have nostrils, good eyes and large openings to their ears.

The basic design of a lizard is very simple and virtually the same in all species. It consists of a head followed by the front pair of legs, then the long trunk or body, the second pair of legs and the long tail trailing behind.

Their eyes are normally situated on either side of the head. Lizard's ears are simple holes covered by a thin, almost *transparent* scale.

Lizards don't possess flaps of skin around their ears like we have to make the sound louder, but some do have two or three overhanging scales to protect them.

Lizards breathe through a pair of nostrils on the end of the snout just above the mouth. They don't use their nostrils for smelling as we would – instead they use their tongue and 'taste' their way around. If you watch a lizard carefully you'll notice that it spends a lot of time flicking its tongue in and out of its mouth (like a snake). It is literally tasting the air or ground, testing it for food, water, a mate or possible danger.

Lizards are covered in scales – similar to a fish's scales and made of the same sort of material as our own hair and fingernails. They protect its body and prevent it from drying out. In order to grow, the lizard occasionally has to shed the hard outer layer of its skin, as the new scales grow underneath. These new scales also help the lizard to keep clean and rid itself of any *parasites* such as ticks or mites.

This anole lizard is shedding its skin in several large pieces.

The lizard's tail

A lizard's tail is very important for a whole variety of reasons. To the lizards that live in the jungle and move about the branches, a tail is very useful for balancing. Iguanas, basilisks and anoles all have very long tails and spend most of their lives in trees. Iguanas spend most of the day sitting on branches above rivers, ready to jump into the water below at the first sign of danger. Their long tails are very useful here, too. An iguana swims by holding its front and hind legs alongside its body and waving its tail from side to side – a little like an eel. Most lizards can swim like this and one type, the Marine Iguana from the Galapagos Islands, has a thick, deep tail so it can swim against the waves.

Some lizards use their tail as a weapon. Monitor lizards from Africa, Asia and Australia have very long, whiplike tails three or four times the length of their body. If anything attacks them, they flick it round just like a whip and can inflict very painful wounds. Some desert-living species, such as the mastigures, use their tails in the same way. Although it's a lot shorter, the mastigure's tail is armed with very sharp spines for extra effect.

Chameleons have a very special tail – it is *prehensile* and the chameleon uses it as a fifth limb as it climbs through the trees where it lives. It can actually hang by its tail alone to reach out for another twig. When it's not in use, the chameleon coils up its tail just like a catherine wheel. Many tree-living lizards have prehensile tails, including the little Elegant Geckoes from New Zealand and the Prehensile-tailed Skink from the Solomon Islands.

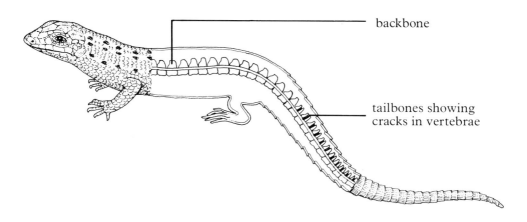

backbone

tailbones showing
cracks in vertebrae

The lizard's amazing tail with its 'cracked' bones which allow it to break off easily in case of danger.

This Green Day Gecko is growing a new tail after shedding its old one.

But perhaps the most important way in which a lizard uses its tail is by losing it! Almost all lizards are able to shed their tails. Only those whose tails are too important to lose – such as the chameleons – keep them permanently. When a lizard is being chased by a *predator,* the first thing that may be caught is its tail. Every bone in the tail has a crack in it so that, with a quick twist of its muscles, the lizard is able to break the bone and its tail drops off. The shed tail actually continues to wriggle for several minutes, drawing the attention of the predator. While its tail is being eaten, the lizard can escape to safety and grow a whole new tail – although it's never quite as perfect as the original one. Apart from a few snakes and the odd salamander, lizards are the only animals that are able to shed their tails.

Most lizards have very good eyesight.

The lizard's eye

Lizards in general have very good eyesight. In the jungle they are constantly on the lookout for food and possible danger. They will probably be able to see you long before you spot them and will scuttle away and hide. Only by moving slowly and quietly will you be able to watch them.

Most lizards have, in fact, not two but three eyes. The third eye, or *pineal eye* as it's known, is very small and is usually on top of the head facing skywards. The lizard can't really see through it, but uses it to measure sunlight – very important to an animal that relies on the sun to keep warm.

Geckoes are active at night and need their large, powerful eyes to see, often in complete darkness. They are among the few lizards that don't have eyelids, although they do have very big eyes. Instead, their eyes are protected by a large, clear scale, a little like a contact lens. While a gecko is asleep during the day, the *pupil* of the eye closes to form a narrow slit. When it's hunting at night, the pupil opens up to let in as much light as possible. Even though the gecko has no eyelids, it can still open and close its eyes.

The gecko's eye is large and powerful – ideal for seeing at night.

The strangest of all lizard eyes belong to the chameleon. A chameleon is active during the day and moves slowly through the trees, picking off insects with its long sticky tongue. Its eyes are placed at the end of cones, but the amazing thing is that each eye can move in any direction at any one time. While its left eye is looking forwards, perhaps at an insect, its right eye can be swivelling around elsewhere looking out for danger.

When the chameleon sees an insect, both eyes point straight ahead, providing the lizard with *stereoscopic* sight. It can now judge exactly how far away the insect is, and is able to pick it off with its long tongue.

Some burrowing lizards are almost completely blind. They spend almost all their lives in underground tunnels or termite nests where there is no light at all. Their eyes have *degenerated* and have become covered over by skin. They find their way around in the dark by smell, using their sensitive tongues.

The chameleon's eyes are set in turrets that can move in any direction.

The chameleon's hands and feet are designed to grasp branches.

Movement

The vast majority of lizards have two pairs of legs and anyone who's tried to catch one, knows just how quickly a lizard can run. Lizards of open country, such as the monitors, have powerful, thick legs which hold their bodies well off the ground. Monitors are excellent runners and their powerful claws enable them to climb trees and termite mounds.

Tree-living lizards, such as iguanas and basilisks, have long slender legs that are useful for jumping between branches. Basilisks are also among the few lizards that are able to lift the front end of their bodies well off the ground and run on their hind legs. This is called 'bipedal locomotion'. The basilisk can run so fast in this way that it can actually run over the surface of a river or stream. That is why it's known to many Central Americans as the 'Jesus Christ' lizard. The unrelated Sail-fin Lizard of Indonesia also lives in trees around rivers. It, too, can run on water for short distances and has a special fringe of scales along the sides of the toes on its hind feet to help it.

The gecko's foot has millions of hair-like scales that help it grip to any surface – in this case, smooth glass.

The most remarkable feet belong to the geckoes which are found throughout the tropics. They live in desert areas and even in houses as well as in the jungle trees. Not only can a gecko run up a wall with ease, but it can also walk up windows and even upside down across the ceiling. The secret lies on the soles of its feet. Geckoes' feet have four or five toes and each one is flattened to form a pad. The underside of each pad is covered by hundreds of thousands of tiny hair-like scales. The hairs are branched like a tree and each branch ends in a flattened disc. These discs cling on to any tiny cracks and ridges on the surface on which the gecko is walking, even though it may appear to be perfectly smooth.

There are also many types of lizard that have no legs at all. The Slow-worm for instance is neither a worm nor slow. It may look like a snake, but it is in fact a legless lizard. It can move very quickly using the same movements as a snake, twisting and weaving through the undergrowth, its long body and tail pushing against anything it touches. Some of the jungle-living legless lizards, such as amphisbaenians, are burrowers and spend their entire life in the moist warm soil. They move through the soil just like earthworms, concertinaing their bodies up tight and then pushing them forward.

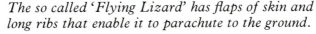

The so called 'Flying Lizard' has flaps of skin and long ribs that enable it to parachute to the ground.

Most lizards, like this gecko, eat insects.

Food and feeding

Around the world lizards, feed on a whole variety of things but most of them are insectivorous. They eat flies, crickets, caterpillars, beetles, grubs and probably anything else small enough to swallow. A few species are herbivorous and eat only plants, fruit and flowers. The Green Iguana of Central and South America is a good example. It's very large, almost six feet (2 metres) in length. When they're very small, Green Iguanas eat insects as well as plants but, as they grow, they feed entirely on leaves and fruit. A close relation – the Marine Iguana of the Galapagos Islands, feeds entirely on a particular type of seaweed that it has to dive for.

The big monitor lizards are both predators and *scavengers*. They will eat small mammals, such as mice and rats, birds, snakes, other lizards and they're particularly fond of eggs. The African Nile Monitor regularly feeds on crocodile eggs. Monitors are large lizards reaching six to nine feet (2-3 metres) and will tear the flesh from dead animals with their very sharp teeth.

Green Iguanas are vegetarian, feeding on leaves, flowers and fruit.

The Caiman Lizard of South America has blunt, rounded teeth designed to crush the shells of its favourite food – snails. Once a shell has been crushed, the pieces are spat out and the soft body is swallowed. Some lizards are very particular about their choice of food. The little flying lizards of Indonesia feed almost entirely on ants and the Australian Thorny Devil eats termites.

Some lizards sit and wait for their *prey* to come nearby while others actively go out and hunt for it, often tracking it down by sight and smell. Once seen, the prey is chased and seized in the lizard's jaws before being crushed and swallowed. The chameleon's long sticky tongue is well known. This strange, flattened lizard with conical eyes moves through the branches of the trees waiting for an insect to land nearby. When it does, the chameleon takes aim and shoots out its sticky tongue with remarkable speed, catches and swallows it. One species, Meller's Chameleon from Malawi, is so big – almost two feet (60cm) – that it can even eat small birds.

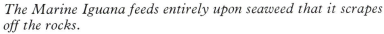

The Marine Iguana feeds entirely upon seaweed that it scrapes off the rocks.

A male anole lizard displays his vivid throat fan to a rival.

Finding a mate

Although most lizards have ears, only a very few are able to make a sound. Instead, they rely on *visual* signals to communicate with each other. Lizards are usually solitary animals, so every breeding season the males have to go about the business of attracting a female. Normally male lizards are much more brightly coloured than females so they can easily be seen in the gloom of the jungle.

In some species the male is larger than the female, in others the female is larger than the male, and in some they are about the same size.

As well as being brightly coloured, some males have crests, flaps or throat fans to make themselves look more impressive. The male Plumed Basilisk from Central America has a large crest on top of his head and a fin along his back and tail. This makes him look much bigger then he really is and also more attractive to a female. The closely related, but much smaller, anole lizards live in the same jungle areas. At only a few inches (cms) long, they're a lot smaller than the three-foot (1-metre) basilisks. Normally it's difficult to tell a male and female anole apart, but during *courtship* the male displays a throat fan that's normally hidden under his chin. The fan is often much bigger than the anole's head and is beautifully coloured. Depending on the species it can be red, orange, yellow, or pink. It's easily seen amid the green leaves of the trees where the anole lives, especially when he starts to bob his head up and down. As well as using his fan to attract a female, the male anole also uses it to drive off any other males in his area.

The male flying lizards of South-east Asia also have a similar throat fan although they're not related to the anoles. They have very long ribs with thin skin in between which they can spread out to the size of a saucer. This makes a very effective parachute and, although the flying lizard doesn't actually 'fly', it does glide very effectively from tree to tree. When a male lands on a new tree, the first thing he does is to display his bright yellow throat fan or 'dewlap' to advertise his presence to other males or any females in the area.

Among the few lizards that DO make a noise, are the little house geckoes of Africa and Asia. They're very popular with tourists who find them running around the walls and ceiling of hotel rooms at night. Both males and females make high-pitched clicking sounds to one another and so are often known as 'chit-chats'.

Male agamas are very brightly coloured – females are usually a dull brown.

The eggs of the Bearded Dragon are laid in shallow holes in the ground.

Eggs

There are two ways in which lizards can reproduce. Some lay eggs which hatch out several months later, while others keep the eggs inside their bodies and the young lizards hatch either immediately, or just after they are laid. This second type are called 'live-bearing' lizards. But the vast majority of lizards lay eggs. Unlike their close relatives, the amphibians, which have to lay their eggs in or near water, reptiles lay their eggs on land. They are able to do this because young lizards inside the eggs are prevented from drying out by a protective shell just like a bird's egg. Some lizards, such as geckoes, have an eggshell very similar to a bird's. It is made of chalk and very brittle. But the shell of most lizard eggs is quite soft and leathery. These eggs can actually soak up water from their surroundings and expand. So within a few hours of being laid the lizard's eggs have grown two or even three times in size.

Lizards usually lay their eggs in holes scraped in the ground, under stones, in rotting vegetation or even in termite mounds. The *embryo*

After about three months the egg is ready to hatch.

The head appears first and . . .

. . . the lizard takes its first breath.

The lizard wriggles free leaving its leathery eggshell behind.

inside the egg needs warmth in order to grow, so the lizards choose a sunny place to lay them. Once they have been laid, most lizards have nothing further to do with their eggs – they are simply left to hatch. It normally takes two or three months for reptile eggs to hatch; the warmer the nest site, the sooner they hatch. The hatching lizard has a special 'egg tooth' on the end of its snout which it uses to rip open the leathery shell and free itself. This is the only time in its life it will need the 'egg tooth' so, after a few days, the lizard sheds its skin and the 'tooth' is lost.

The tiny lizard is able to feed and fend for itself as soon as it has hatched. Depending on the species, it can take anything from a few months to several years before it reaches full adult size. It is certainly possible for lizards that live in jungles to lay several clutches of eggs a year instead of the normal one clutch laid by other lizards. No matter what time of year they hatch, the baby lizards will always find plenty of food to enable them to grow very quickly.

A newly-hatched Bearded Dragon, a perfect replica of its parents.

19

The Shingleback Lizard from Australia gives birth to two, very large young.

Live young

Instead of laying eggs, some lizards keep them within their bodies until they hatch and then give birth to live, fully-formed young. As there is no need for a protective covering, the eggshell is replaced by a very thin, almost transparent envelope.

There are some advantages to giving birth to live young rather than laying eggs. Lizard eggs are good to eat and many of those laid in the ground or under stones get eaten. Many animals will eat them; small mammals, birds, insects and other reptiles. So by keeping them inside her body, the female lizard is protecting the eggs from predators.

The female lizard is also acting as a mobile *incubator*, taking her eggs with her wherever she goes. When the sun shines, she spreads her body out in the sun and at the same time exposes her eggs to the warmth so that the embryos can develop normally.

In the jungle, many species of skink are live-bearers, as are many types of snake. The only disadvantage of being a live-bearer is that the female has to carry the eggs for three months or even longer. An egg-laying lizard could have laid many clutches of eggs during this time, although it's likely that not many would survive. Also, carrying eggs around inside her makes the female lizard very large, so she may not be able to escape quickly enough if a snake or other predator should see her. But whether lizards lay eggs or give birth to live young, there are still plenty of animals in the jungle that would readily make a meal of the tiny offspring.

A newly-born Jackson's Chameleon, one of a dozen, walks over its parent's head.

A harmless Shingleback Lizard displays its large pink mouth and bright blue tongue to frighten off predators.

Enemies and defence

Lizards are eaten by a whole variety of animals. Birds, mammals, large frogs and even some of the larger spiders prey on them. Smaller lizards are often eaten by bigger ones and there are some species of snake that feed only on lizards. Nocturnal lizards, such as geckoes, fall prey to owls and mammals that hunt at night. Some large species, such as the Australian goannas and the South American iguanas, are eaten by humans. (Iguanas taste a little like chickens!)

During the day, lizards rely on their good eyesight and speed to escape from their enemies. If they are caught, they can often rely on their remarkable ability to shed their tails to escape from predators. At night, day-living lizards hide away in a hole in the ground, under a large stone or log or under the bark of a tree. Nocturnal lizards do the same thing during the day.

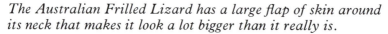

The Australian Frilled Lizard has a large flap of skin around its neck that makes it look a lot bigger than it really is.

An Ameiva is fatally bitten by a Hog-nosed Viper.

Large lizards, like the iguanas, spend the day sitting on the branches of trees overhanging rivers. Should a predator come too close, the iguana simply drops into the water below and swims away to escape the danger. The lizard usually returns to the same branch on the same tree, some time later.

Many species of lizard have scales that are shaped to form spines as a protection. Others have flaps of skin either under their chins, on top of their heads or around their necks. When danger threatens, these are spread out to make the lizard look much bigger than it really is. The predator then decides that this creature is much too big to eat and so leaves it alone.

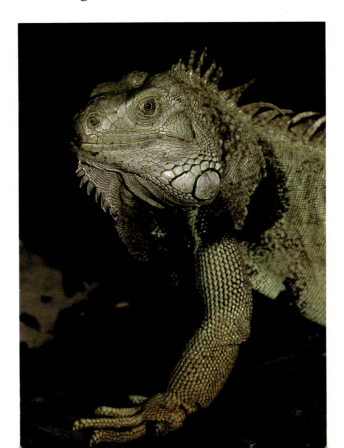

The Green Iguana has a large eye-like scale on its cheek and a flap under its chin that makes its head look twice as big.

23

This Leaf-tailed Gecko blends in perfectly with the bark of the tree.

Camouflage

One of the best means of defence against being eaten is to try and avoid being seen at all. Many animals blend in with their backgrounds so well that it's impossible to see them unless they start to move. Many lizards are *camouflaged* in this way and the jungle is one of the best places to find them – if you can see them! Many species of gecko live on the trunks of trees and are perfectly camouflaged to blend in with the bark. The Leaf-tailed Geckoes of the forests of Eastern Australia are a very good example. Not only are they coloured to match their background, but they are also very flattened, especially their tails, so as not to stand out from the bark or throw any shadows during the day.

The little anole lizards of the Americas are long and thin and normally lie along a branch to escape being seen. They are also able to change their colour from brown to green; brown for when they are on the branches of trees and green when they are moving among the leaves. Because of this ability to change colour, they're often known as 'American Chameleons'. The true chameleons, though, live only in Southern Europe, Africa and Asia. When it comes to the art of camouflage, these lizards are among the

This little anole exactly matches the colours of a leaf.

best examples. They are able to change their colour to match almost any background. They can't, of course, match the patterns and colours of a tartan rug or a chess board, but they can merge in with almost any natural background.

The secret of the chameleon's ability to change colour lies in special *cells* in its skin. Each one is like a tiny plastic bag filled with clear liquid. The liquid is full of tiny dark particles. When the particles are all clumped in one place, the chameleon is very pale in colour but, when they are spread out throughout the liquid, the lizard is dark. The chameleon is able to control exactly where the particles are, and by having several layers of these cells of different colours, it can change to any shade of colour very quickly.

However, there is no point in being well camouflaged if you are constantly on the move. Most of the best-camouflaged lizards move very little and, when they do, it's usually very slowly. When a chameleon walks along a branch it sways backwards and forwards just like a leaf blowing in the wind. The Helmeted Iguanid from Costa Rica looks like part of a branch; it often sits in the same position for days and days, safe from the eyes of predators and just waiting to snap up any passing insect.

Chameleons can change their colour to match almost any background.

Geckoes make themselves useful by eating moths and mosquitoes in houses in the tropics.

Lizards and people

Unless we deliberately go out to look for lizards, it's only rarely that people and lizards cross paths. House geckoes are probably the only lizards that actually live near us. They live around our houses throughout the warm tropics, spending the day sleeping behind furniture and wall hangings and emerging after dark to hunt for insects. They do house owners a good service by eating the flies and mosquitoes that come in at night, attracted by the lights. The only time they cause alarm is when they fall off the ceiling while hunting, and land with a slight bump on the carpet or bed. But some lizards can be real pests as far as humans are concerned. Monitors will break into hen houses to steal chickens and eggs, tearing open the wire mesh with their very strong claws. Lizards in the Canary Islands are often poisoned and shot by fruit growers. As well as insects, these lizards eat tomatoes, grapes and other fruit, and like the fruit, they thrive in the damp, sunny conditions.

There are, of course, many species of lizard that are hunted by humans. The Tegu, a three-foot (1-metre) long lizard from South America, and

In Trinidad it is believed that if you are bitten or even touched by a Twenty-four Hours Lizard, then you only have a day to live. It is, however, completely harmless.

Green Iguanas are a favourite food of people living in Central America.

monitors from Africa and Asia, are hunted for their skins and flesh. There are even plans to farm Tegus commercially for their skins. Goannas have long been hunted by Australian Aborigines for their tasty flesh, while iguanas are relished by the Indians that live in the jungles of Central America. Even today, iguana is often served as a snack in many of the roadside bars in Costa Rica and Panama.

Throughout the world there are also many lizards that are actually feared by humans – even though they may be very small. In Trinidad the Twenty-four Hours Lizard gets its name from the mistaken belief that if one bites, or even just touches you, then you'll die within twenty-four hours. Chameleons are looked upon with dread by the people of many African countries even though they are completely harmless.

The Gila Monster and Beaded Lizard which live in the southern part of the United States and Mexico are the only poisonous lizards known. But the most fearsome lizard of all is the Komodo Dragon from the tiny island of Komodo in Indonesia. This twelve-foot (4-metre) giant, the largest lizard alive, is a type of monitor which kills and eats deer and goats. There is at least one record of a person having been killed by a Komodo Dragon.

The bright colours of the poison-arrow frogs warn predators that they contain deadly substances.

Friends and neighbours

Lizards share their jungle home with many other animals. The trees and other plants provide food and shelter for thousands of insects, other reptiles, birds and mammals. Under every rotting log lying on the ground, millipedes, centipedes, worms, spiders, beetles and grubs are all taking shelter with the lizards, frogs and snakes. Under the bark of the trees, cockroaches sleep during the day alongside the geckoes. Between the tangled roots, nocturnal toads and snakes lurk, waiting for nightfall when they'll emerge to hunt among the fallen leaves. The dead leaves are the home of tiny lizards, such as skinks, that thrive in the soggy conditions. So do tiny poison-arrow frogs, the size of a person's fingernail and brightly coloured to warn predators that they have poisonous skin. Both the frogs and skinks feed on the thousands of tiny crickets and springtails that spring up around your feet as you walk through the dense forest. Tortoises amble along the floor of the jungle looking for fallen fruit and mushrooms, and terrapins bask on logs on the banks of rivers sixty feet (20 metres) below the iguanas in the tree tops.

The Clearwing Moth looks more like a large bee than a moth.

Many animals share the same food as the lizards. Frogs and toads feed mainly on insects. Monkeys spend the day, like the iguanas, eating leaves, flowers and fruit. Very few of the many species of birds that live in the jungle will harm lizards. The vast majority will live quite happily side by side with most types of lizard. Bats, too, present no threat to the reptiles. They feed mainly on winged insects and often share their daytime roost with geckoes and snakes.

Virtually every lizard has other animals living on its skin and scales. They are tiny parasites called ticks and mites that feed mainly on the lizard's blood, just like a dog's fleas. They don't really harm the lizard – as long as it stays healthy, they stay healthy. You need a magnifying glass to see because they are usually the size of a pin-head and often bright red in colour. They are probably the closest and smallest of the lizard's neighbours in the jungle.

Huge millipedes patrol the forest floor feeding on dead leaves and other vegetable matter.

Life in the jungle

In many respects lizards that live in the jungle have quite an easy life. Tropical forest trees have leaves all year round; they don't shed them in the autumn like many of ours do. So there is always plenty of food in the form of vegetation, or insects that feed on the vegetation, for the lizards to eat. So food isn't usually a problem. Nor is water, because these forests only survive in areas of plenty of water, even during the driest times of year. And, as these forests only grow in the tropical areas of the world, keeping warm isn't a problem either, for the lizards or for their eggs. The soil in the jungle is warm enough for the eggs to develop and there's no shortage of nesting places. The only problem with living in an *environment* that's so favourable and rich in plant and animal life is that,

Food chain

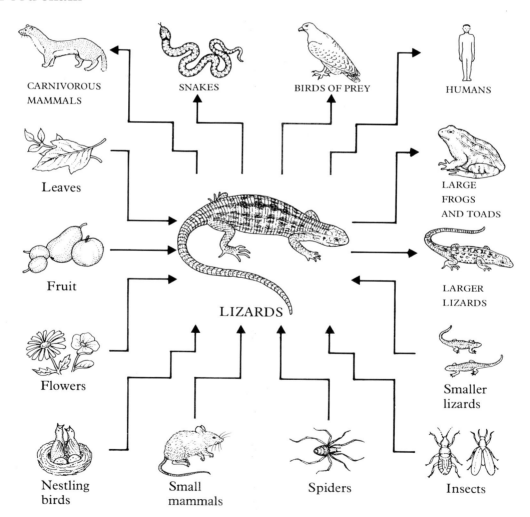

CARNIVOROUS MAMMALS

SNAKES

BIRDS OF PREY

HUMANS

Leaves

LARGE FROGS AND TOADS

Fruit

LARGER LIZARDS

LIZARDS

Flowers

Smaller lizards

Nestling birds

Small mammals

Spiders

Insects

Ameivas sun themselves along river banks and in forest clearings.

while there's plenty of food for the lizards, there are also plenty of other animals just waiting to make a meal of them. Snakes abound in these warm tropical forests and besides frogs, birds and small mammals, many of them also eat lizards. In fact some species feed entirely on lizards and nothing else.

The smaller skinks get eaten by large frogs, toads and even spiders while the geckoes are often devoured by nocturnal mammals. Even the large iguanas and basilisks aren't safe in the tree tops. They can be snatched from the branches by large birds of prey and, if they do leap to the relative safety of the river, there are always boas and other large snakes waiting for them.

But by far the biggest threat to these jungle lizards comes from people. Our demand for timber means that these rich tropical forests are being chopped down at an alarming rate all over the world. Many of the lizards, as well as all the other animals that live there, are faced with extinction. A lizard that's camouflaged to look like the bark of a tree or a branch or a dead leaf won't last very long on bare soil.

Glossary

camouflage :   animal disguise – the way in which an animal hides by blending in with its background **24, 25, 31**

cells :   the tiny basic building blocks of all life **25**

courtship :   display or behaviour to attract a mate **16**

degenerated :   reduced in size, often through lack of use **11**

embryo :   the developing animal inside the egg **18, 21**

environment :   the natural surroundings **30**

equator :   the imaginary line that runs around the centre of the world **4**

habitat :   the natural home of any plant or animal **5**

herbivorous :   feeding on plants **3, 14**

hibernate :   to sleep over winter **3**

incubator :   a device for keeping eggs warm so that they will hatch **21**

insectivorous :   feeding on insects **3, 14**

nocturnal :   active only at night **3, 22, 28, 31**

parasite :   an animal or plant that lives and feeds on another **7, 29**

pineal eye :   a tiny, third eye on the top of a lizard's head **10**

predator :   an animal that kills and eats other animals **9, 14, 20, 21, 22, 23, 25, 28**

prehensile :   capable of grasping **8**

prey :   an animal that is hunted by another animal for food **15, 22, 31**

pupil :   the hole in the middle of the eye that appears black **10**

reptiles :   a group of animals, including lizards, snakes, crocodiles and tortoises, which are coldblooded and covered in horny scales **3, 6, 18, 19, 20, 28, 29**

scavenger :   an animal that feeds on the left-overs or dead bodies of other animals **14**

species :   a type of animal (or plant) which can interbreed successfully with others of its kind, but not with those of a different type **3, 4, 5, 7, 14, 15, 16, 19, 21, 22, 23, 24, 26, 29, 31**

stereoscopic :   a type of vision in which both eyes point in the same direction so that distances can be judged exactly **11**

temperate :   the cooler regions of the earth between the tropics and the poles **3, 5**

transparent :   clear enough to see through **7, 20**

tropical : (tropics)   relating to the hot areas around the middle of the earth to the north and south of the equator **3, 5, 13, 26, 30, 31**

visual :   by sight **16**

First published in Great Britain 1988
by Methuen Children's Books Ltd
11 New Fetter Lane, London EC4P 4EE
Conceived, designed and produced by Belitha Press Ltd
31 Newington Green, London N16 9PU
Copyright © in this format Belitha Press Ltd 1988
Text © Oxford Scientific Films 1988
Series Editor: Jennifer Coldrey
Scientific Adviser: Dr Gwynne Vevers
Art Director: Treld Bicknell   Design: Naomi Games
ISBN 0 416 06542 2
Printed in Hong Kong by South China Printing Co.

The publishers wish to thank the following for permission to reproduce copyright material: **Oxford Scientific Films Ltd.** for front cover, pp 7 *both*, 9, 15 *above*, 18 *all*, 19 *all*, 20, 24 *below*, 28, 29 *both* and 31 (**Mike Linley**); title page (P. J. Devries); pp 2, 11 *above*, 22 *above* and 26 *below* (J. A. L. Cooke); pp 3, 5, 6 *both*, 16, 22 *below*, 23 *above* and back cover (Michael Fogden); pp 4 and 17 (Anthony Bannister); p 10 (Stephen Dalton); pp 11 *below* and 27 (G. I. Bernard); pp 12 and 14 (P. and W. Ward); p 13 *above* (Breck P. Kent); pp 13 *below*, 21 and 25 (Z. Leszczynski); p 15 *below* (Godfrey Merlin); p 23 *below* (Stuart Bebb); p 24 *above* (Martins Wildlife Films); p 26 *above* (Peter Parks).

The line drawings are by Lorna Turpin.